COMPOSER SHOWCASE
HAL LEONARD STUDENT PIANO LIBRARY

Poetic Moments

8 CHARACTER PIECES FOR PIANO SOLO

BY CHRISTOS TSITSAROS

T0053232

CONTENTS

Original poetry by Christos Tsitsaros

Editor: Margaret Otwell

ISBN 0-634-06349-9

HAL•LEONARD®
CORPORATION
7777 W. BLUEMOUND RD. P.O. BOX 13819 MILWAUKEE, WI 53213

In Australia Contact:
Hal Leonard Australia Pty. Ltd.
22 Taunton Drive P.O. Box 5130
Cheltenham East, 3192 Victoria, Australia
Email: ausadmin@halleonard.com

Visit Hal Leonard Online at
www.halleonard.com

Migrating Bird

– C. T.

As the days of summer wane away,

And you prepare to set off for strange, far-away lands,

Remember the little nest you built over my doorstep.

As the winds carry you aloft,

And the land below slowly fades away,

Look back, and remember:

There is always a warm place for you in my heart.

Migrating Bird

For Aline Andres

Christos Tsitsaros

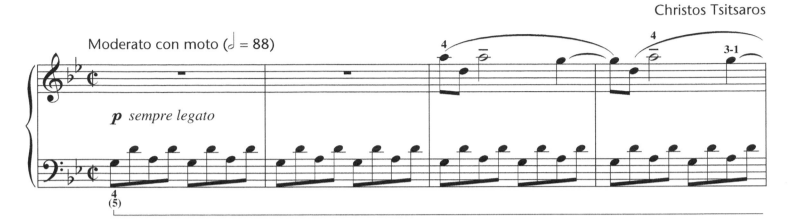

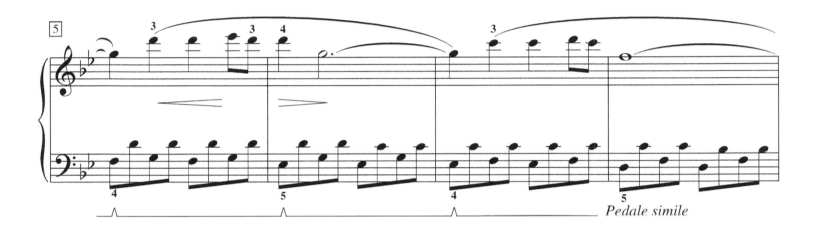

Lullaby

– C. T.

Let the sunshine penetrate your soul through your closed lashes,

Let it keep your heart tender and warm,

Tucked safely away from the worries of the world.

Sleep in the sunshine, little angel; sleep in my arms.

Lullaby

Christos Tsitsaros

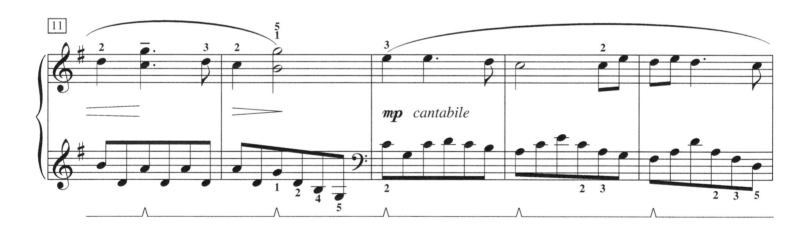

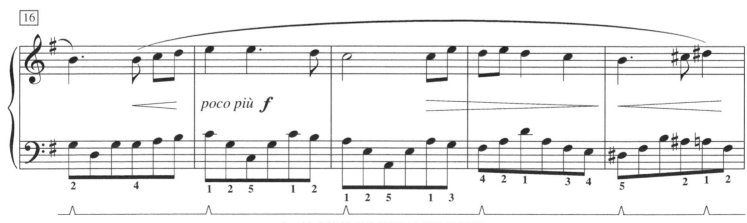

Dance Of The Sprites

– C. T.

There are sprites in the woods in the late afternoon;

They glide through the streams, jump high on the branches.

They whirl in the wind, sing together with joy.

Listen! Can you hear their laughter?

Dance Of The Sprites

Christos Tsitsaros

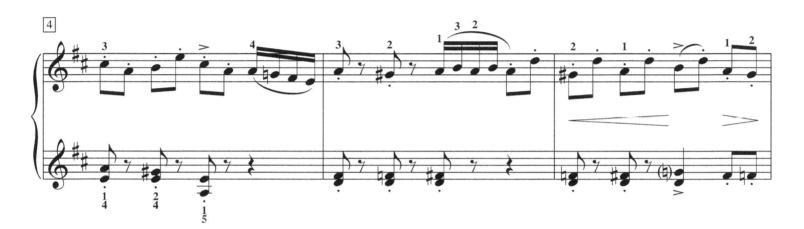

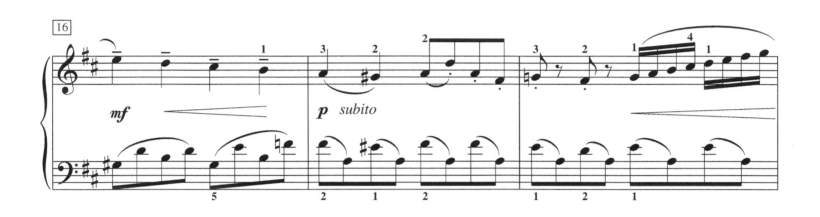

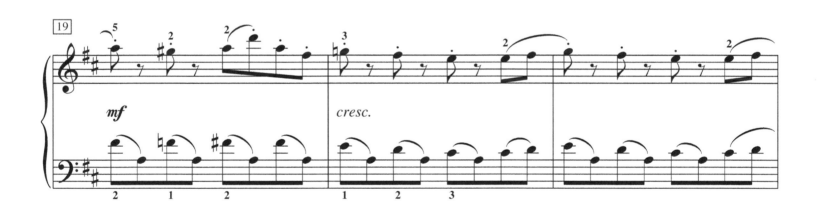

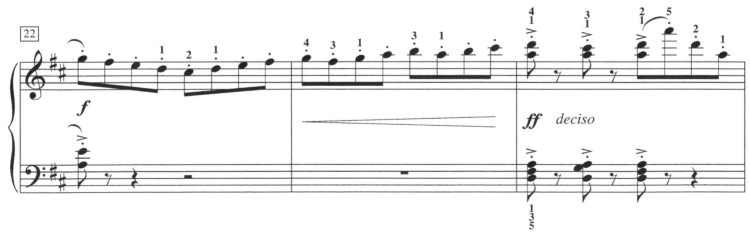

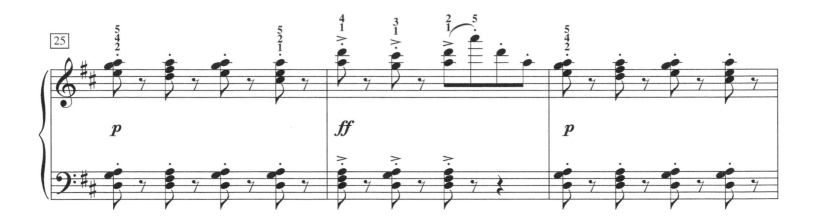

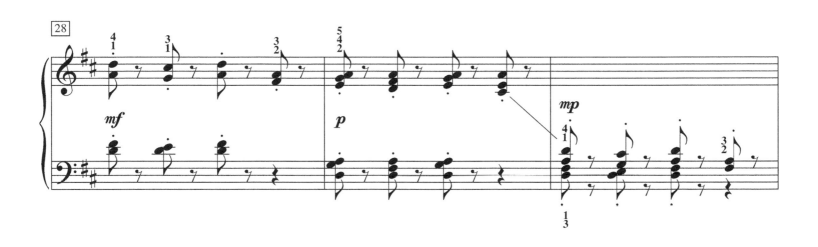

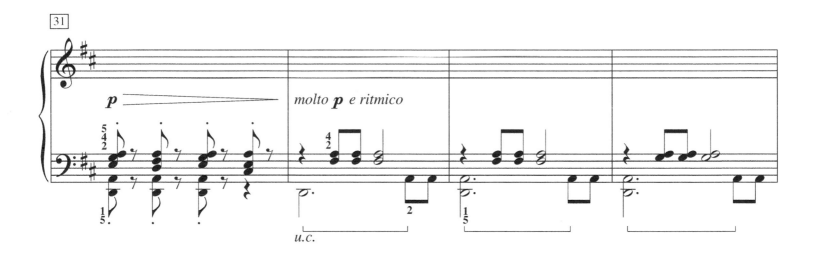

Pedale simile

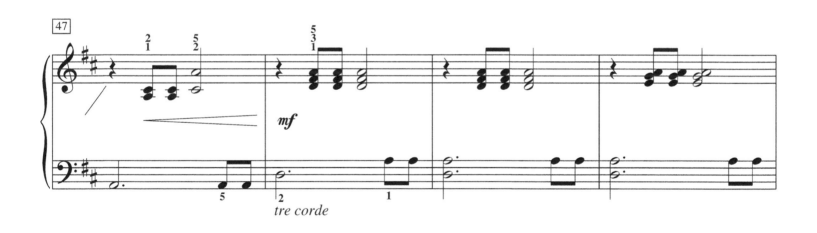

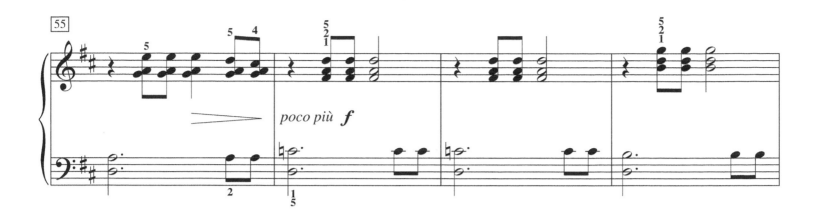

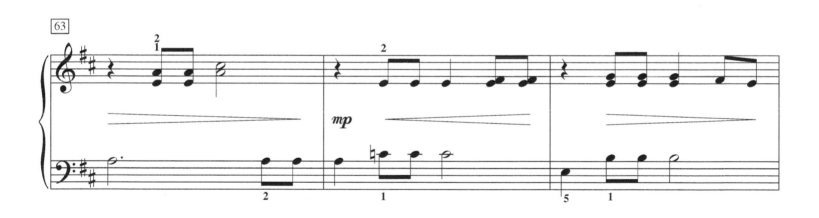

15

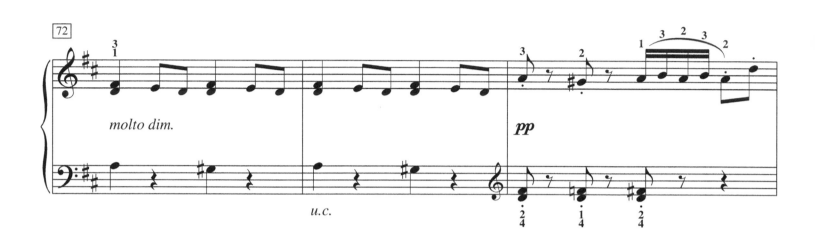

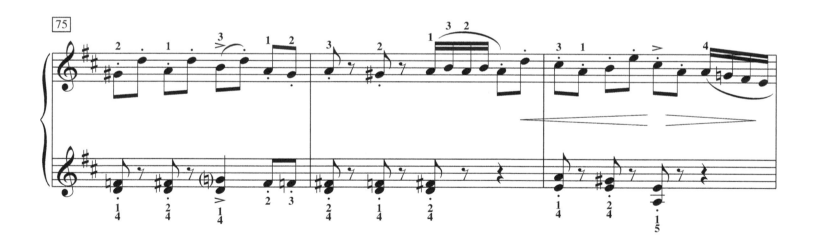

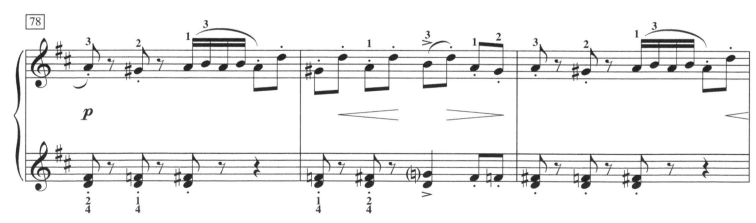

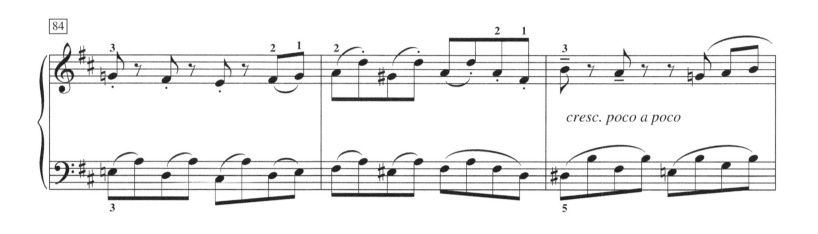

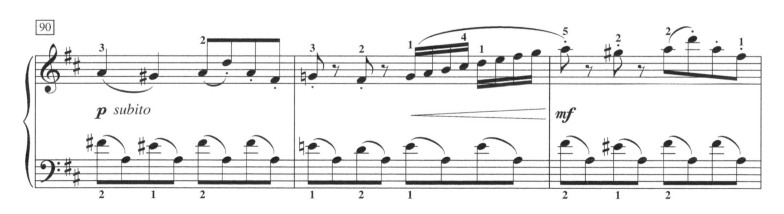

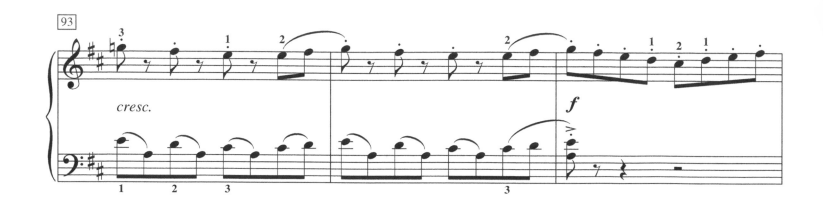

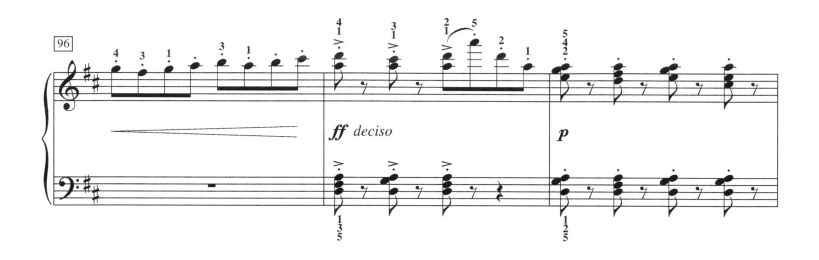

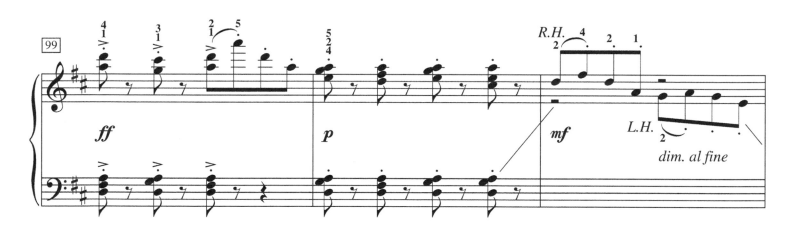

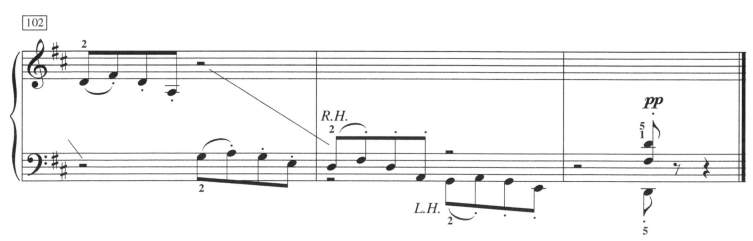

Blues Valsette
(Falling Leaves)

– C. T.

My front yard is covered in a thousand muted colors.

The red-gold leaves are falling, ever so light, feather-like…

I can see them waltzing slowly, lazily.

I long to be one of them, disappear with them,

And return in the spring.

Blues Valsette
(Falling Leaves)

Christos Tsitsaros

Moderato semplice e espressivo (♩. = 56)

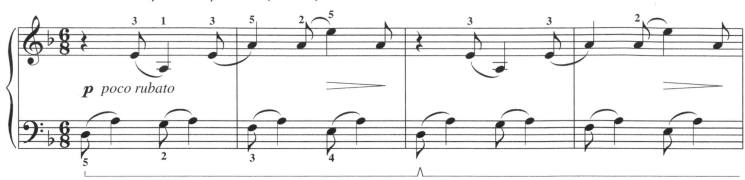

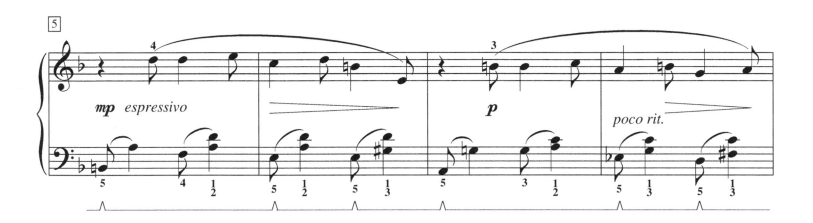

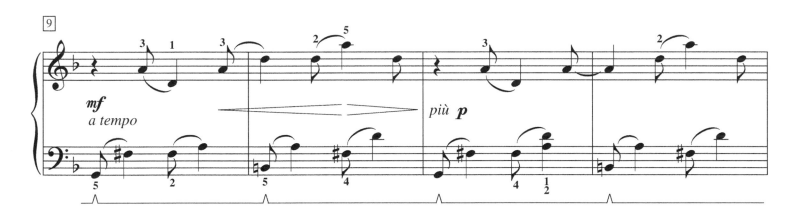

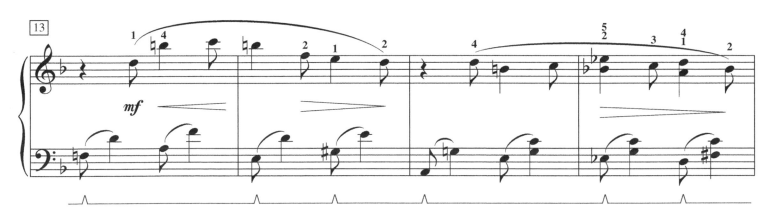

The Little Carousel

– C. T.

In my dream there was this empty carousel,

And I heard a sweet, melancholy tune,

It was turning 'round, as if children were there, having fun,

But I couldn't see them.

Only at the end of my dream,

Did I finally, briefly glimpse someone: It was I.

The Little Carousel

Christos Tsitsaros

Waltz tempo, with a melancholy playfulness ($\bullet$. = 69)

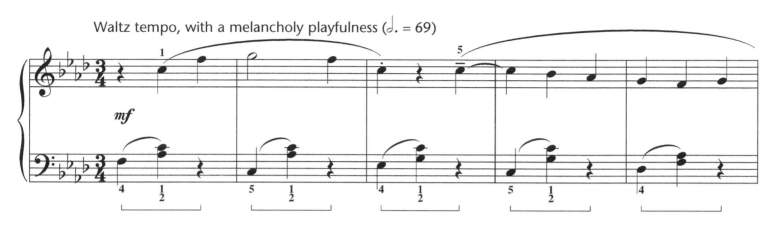

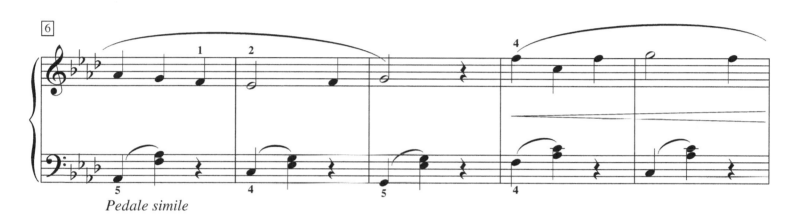

Pedale simile

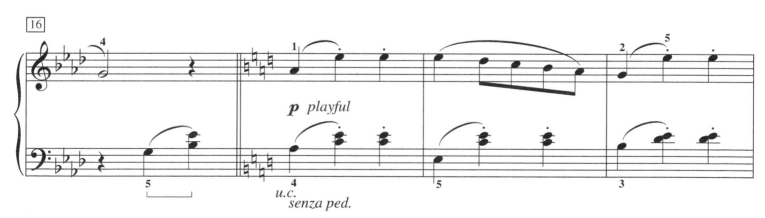

poco più **p**

f

tre corde

Pedale simile

Butterfly Rag

– C. T.

Two butterflies are drawing imaginary lines in the deep blue sky,

Flickering their spotted wings in harmony.

Now they seem drunk; later, in love.

Then, they split away

To appear suddenly anew, right in front of me!

Butterfly Rag

Christos Tsitsaros

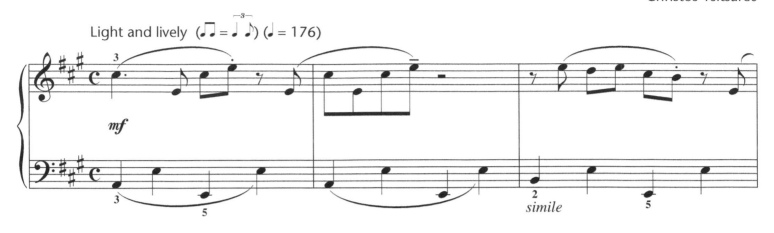

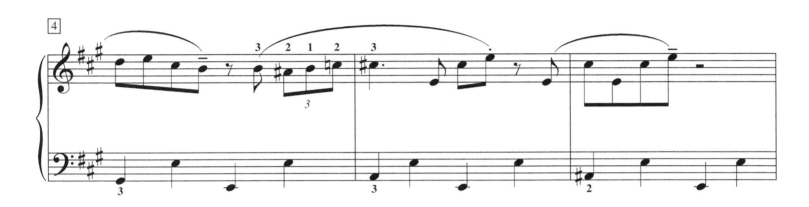

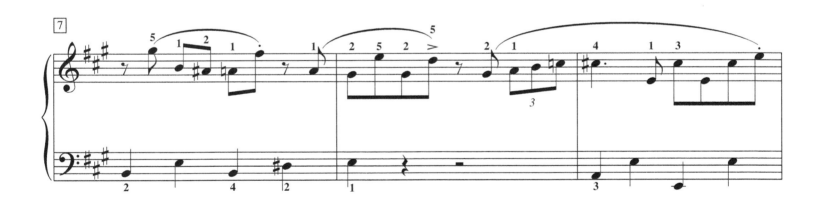

Unfinished Melody

– C. T.

The wind brings to me its song.

It swirls in my head, and carries me away with it.

It's a song I know, one I have heard before.

I try to catch it, hum it, but it's gone with the wind.

Unfinished Melody

Christos Tsitsaros

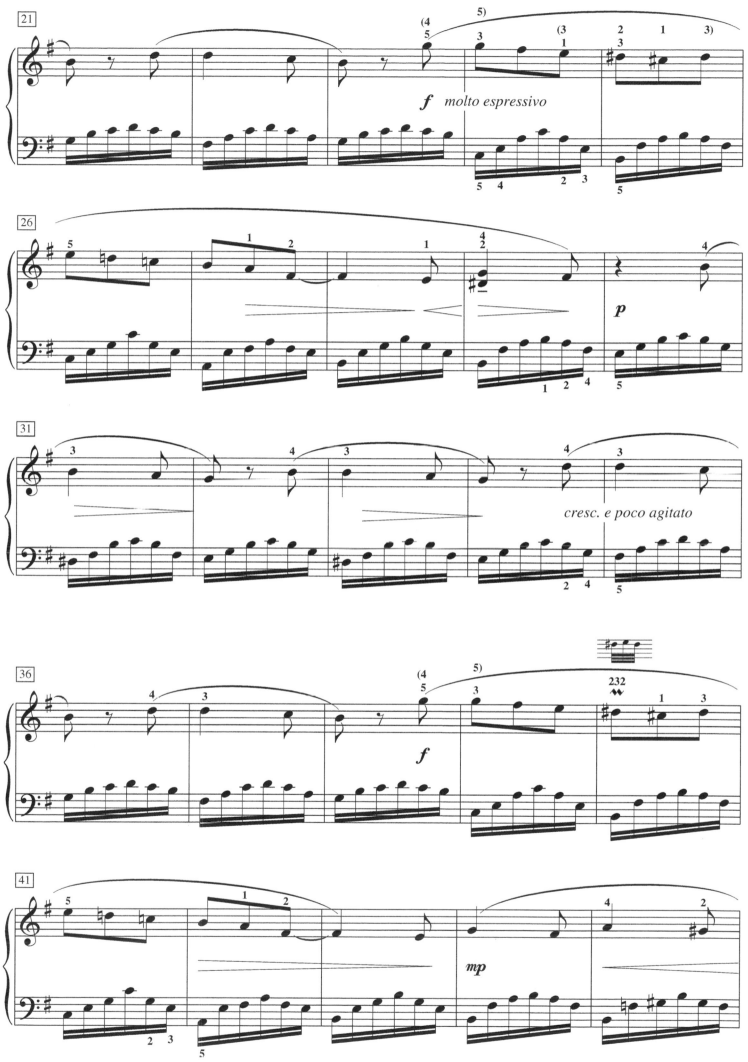

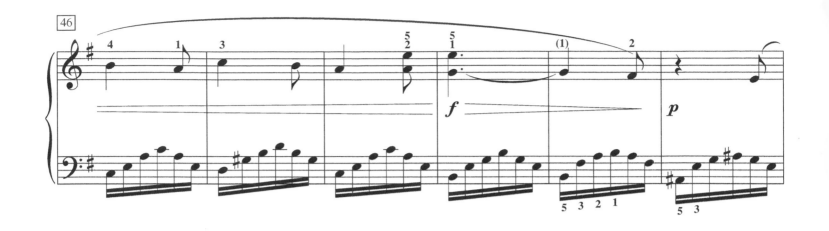

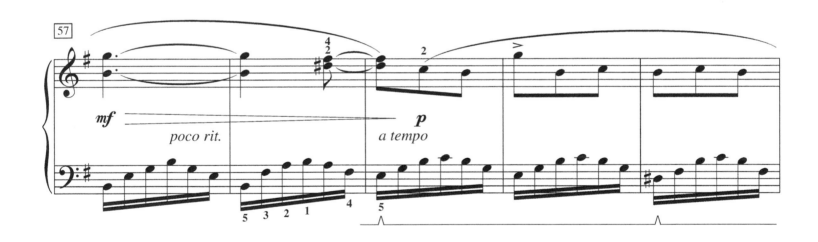

Westbound Train

– C. T.

The train sets out for the far-off West,

I can already see towering mountains;

Hear thunderous hoofbeats of wild horses;

And smell smoky gunfire from an outlaw ambush.

There's a big adventure lying ahead

Involving grand schemes and dangerous deeds...

But, oh! I am in a cinema on a hot Sunday afternoon.

Westbound Train

Christos Tsitsaros